I0188259

COCKROACH HEART

(Un)Requited Love in The Times of Terrorism

B.C. Farbo

The Orph Press LLC | Savannah, Georgia

The Orph Press
LLC
Savannah, Georgia

Poems, Illustrations,
Photographs, and Design
B.C. Farbo

(C) 2019 all rights reserved

www.bcfarbo.com
www.theorphpress.com

ISBN: 978-0-578-49092-2

Contents & Discontents:

To: V.,

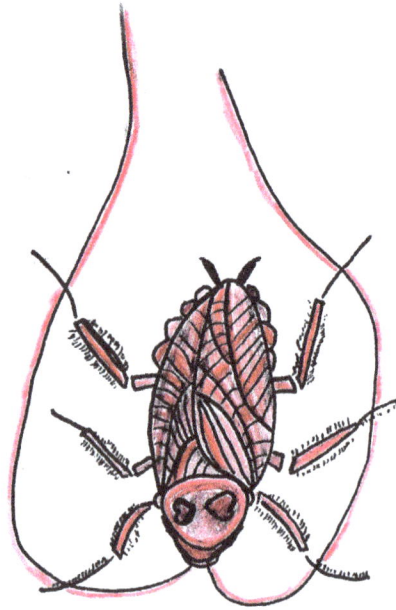

Questions about Mental Sanitation?

Madame Cockroach knows
humans like everything else
are fads to be endured.

I will attempt to stab her with a fork,
as she runs across the dirty bar.

Unfortunately,
she is my heart.

Fortunately,

I miss.

Fairy Shrimp
was born under a New Moon,
ass first.

180 nights that way,
and 185 mornings the other
the color of Smoky Veined Azurite.

During the boring time
before the monsoons came.

When Gods threw lighting,
at the thirsty earth.
off their matchbooks.

To impress femininity
like ornery juveniles
on the Friday Night Make.

Near The Equator of 1984

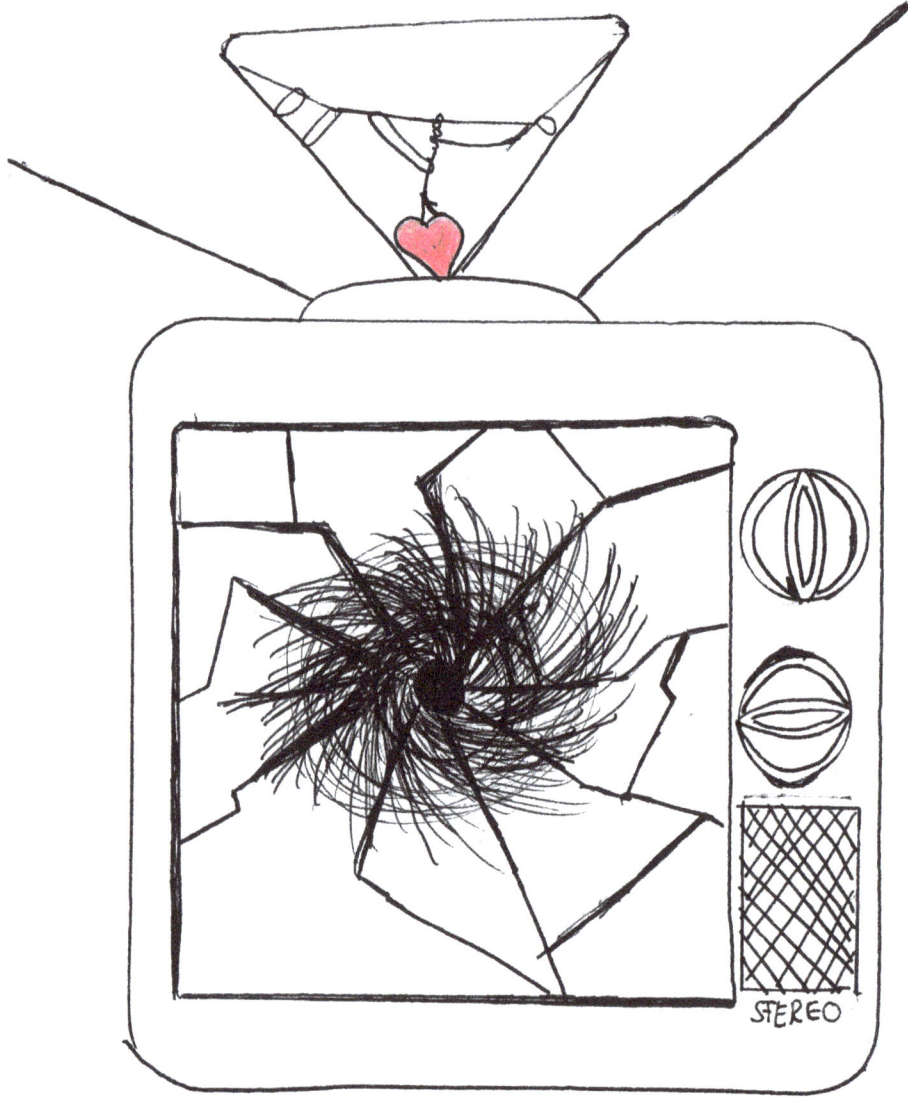

Grace (LESS) land

Babe was told,
go back to sleep.

Victorious,
the neighbors politely marveled.
But not sleepy Babe,
who saw no point,
in Father's love for dead kings.

N
O
W

Parents skirmished,
stayed together,
then   severed.

While her Mama champed
bare toothed for Priscilla's
toe nail clippers
ONLY $19.99 plus S&H.

Divorced too young w/ maxed out
monopoly money,
Father bitterly bidding off the TV...

Point of purchase,
to trim the feathers off,
for her progeny to see,
the chicken skin,
of that chicken shit.

1
2
3

For a single commemorative eyelash
w/ certificate.
Plucked from Elvis's corpse,
as he chilled on the commode floor.

Both thinking they
could level up buying royal relics,
while being devoured by arcade
ghost.

(You! Got. IT. ALL.
Our last quarter on credit!
For that damn machine!
You think you are Lisa Marie?)

Rest Babe in the garish Grace (LESS) land not of your hearts design, for tomorrow it comes down.

It's now or never...

Two Lovers in Asymmetrical Warfare:

Beating down a primitive road she ponders aloud,

"Our lives were never symmetrical.
Yet, I love you with a merciless heart."

The other turns the A.M. dial,

"Hush!!It's OUR song...

Jesus Hammurabi Christ,
Stop! Cleaning your ears with your keys.
EYES! ON! THE! ROAD!"

B-4 All was Fair in Love and War

and Battleship?

Where,
sour/bitter pools,
under the tongue,
dime flavored anticipation.

sweat dripped,
sauntering down
spectacle temple tips

strategy formed,
during rounds of Battleship,
played by the left field foul line,
on a pick-up bed,

under the left ear lobe,
middle finger's length,
from the common carotid artery.

B-4

I am sunk.

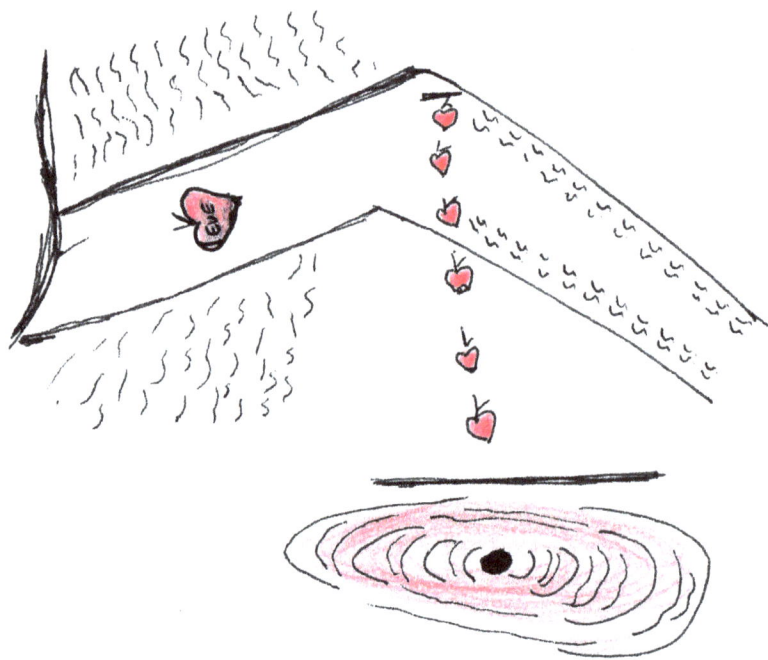

Magdalene:
Age 15 ½
Shaves While Getting the Nerve to Ask

Singular tension,
one toothbrush,
one comb,
one razor,
one corduroy jacket,
National
Blue

Through,
consecrated conduits
wrapped in adventitia,
falling carmine
from a nicked knee
tracing water
into porcelain coolness.

Dismissed
pink wisps
skeleton
down a grimy, solitary
drainpipe.

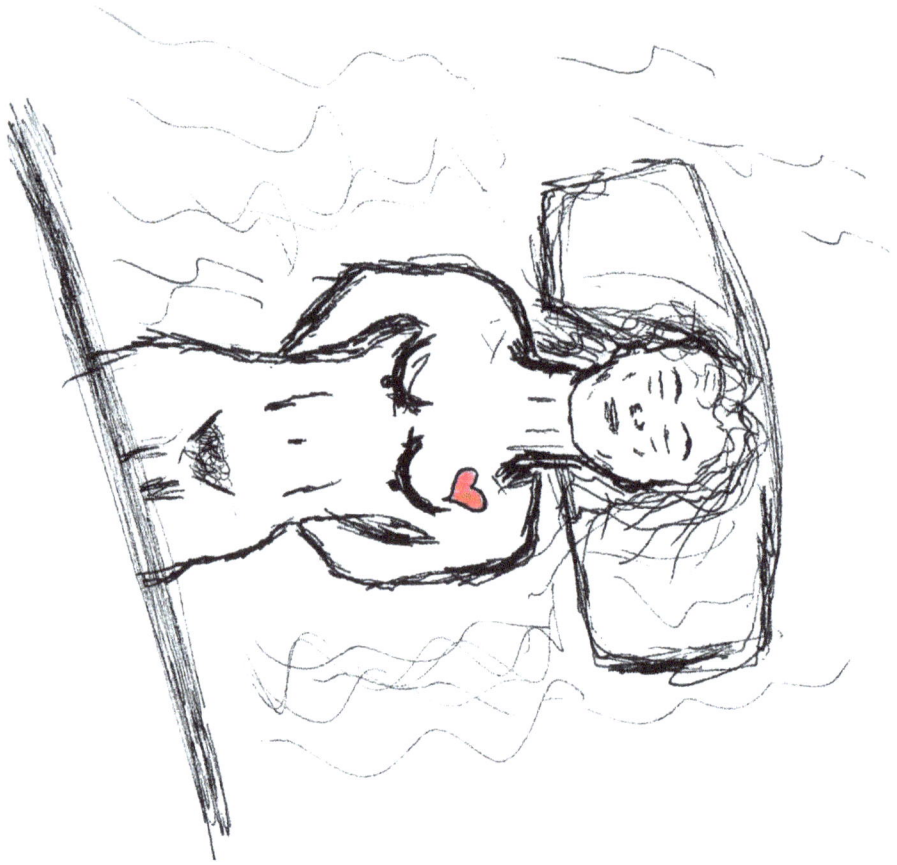

The cake should read...
"Happy 39+1 Sweets"
What won't fit is as follows:

For
14,599
days
and
nights
The
Rains,
rung
Her
bell.

Her
heel
the
disputed
axis
of
the
drowned
rat
earth.

Those
14,599
days
and
nights
mean
zilch....

.

10 AM and the day is unmercifully
faded. It is that sort.

(What was the name of those two?

Like finding that
picture of a crowd,
from a long forgotten
Second Cousin's,
second wedding,
to First Shelly.

Jason

and

Charlotte?

In Sunday best,
bored eyes
looking up,
glazed as reception hams.

Possibly?

Screwed on smiles,
stomach churned,
from the indigestion
of matrimonial line dances
done drunk.

Huh?

10:00 PM and that night remains It
is that sort.

Ones who?)

Let NO Chicken Dance put
asunder...

What GOD has brought together...

To Maintain Stain:
Wash in Hot Water
Tumble Dry

A smart mouthed woman,

who knows she,

never could do good laundry.

Who pops gum,

in attempted crimes against greasy

opulences of ordinary Frito Pie palaces.

Who concedes olives taste of decent sex,

in ways unsavory,

on me like a green corn husk.

Never to be discontinued due to demand,

who blesses in jackpot hickies,

a shade called "Chimayo" her inheritance.

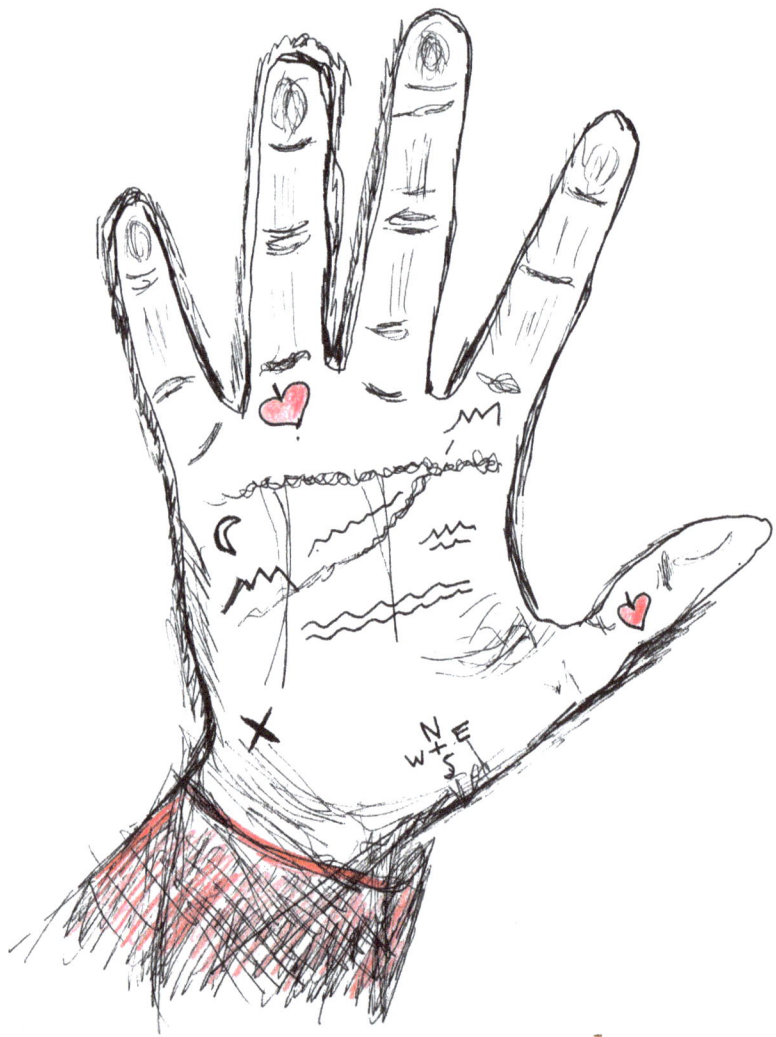

Remember That Love
Song?

Of when
the coldest day
in
Hell
met
and
fell in love
with this worldly life?

                                          Of the

                                          running

                                          thieves

With good
ideas
on paper.

Who
got
cast
away
summarily
from
the sweet by and by.

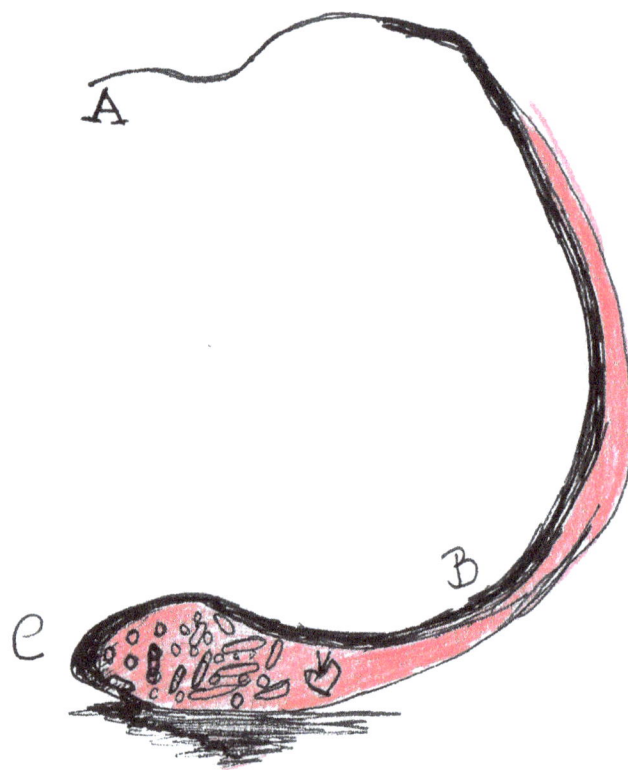

In the meantime...

Wagers
 fail

Promise
        staggers

Lust
wilts

Stress

    remains
    residual

    Pinched
    passions
    like
    a
    Prince Rupert's

    Drop

                    shatter.

Note Left on Receipt at Front Desk
of The Garden of Gethsemane
Motel 6:

-Sins atoned by proxy-

Peter THAT queen
put sword to the
soldier's lover,
and was rebuked.

-No more of this-

The ear was returned, so that
it could hear the good news.

-Bitch is still waiting-

IED/IDP

She did not move from the TV.

                  Round to the head.

Casual
fatality
just
another
small town/
countryside
refugee.

مرداد ۱۳۸۹

جمعه ۱۸

⊙ —

Have a Milkshake!
My Sweet Habibi!

Blind drunk on Tajik Moonshine

Inhaling diesel air incensed and
encased.

Grey haired, handsome, soldier,
brogue of the Orange.

A splintered partner in crime.

Woebegone we sat,
him and I.

Our solid fence posts an
Essex Man,
his reluctant future Brisi Bride.
A driver named Barry.

I spilled my guts on Hajii Jakob
Square.

Lament the Whiteworker's Daughter

She never embroidered latticed wounds
into her body.

The acts of men had done it for her,

one,
ten,
a hundred,
a thousand,

pulled threads at a time
turning her heart into beating lace.

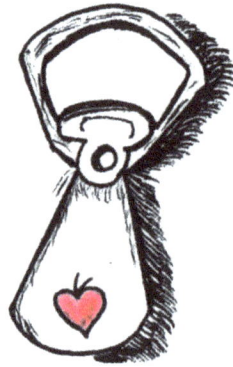

The Bargirl: A Lotus Eater

Sees What Time Has Taken

A Dutchman to the left.   An Irishman to the right

queries....

The Bargirl dead middle at the draft spout

about their "No."

chances...

Everything,
goes
limp.

Except the ability,
to raise a finger,
for one more

that keeps it

down.

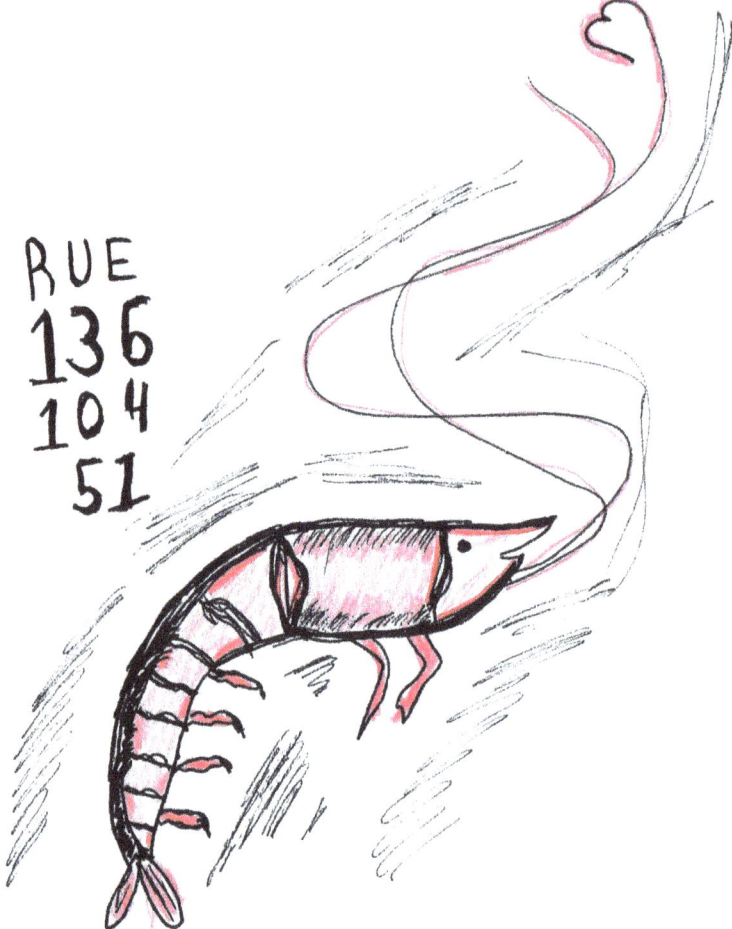

RUE
136
104
51

Rahab on break from
her John hits The Ladies'
Room

The late afternoon light
stumbles through
windows.

A pious sobering up occurs,
as I look for a glass to fill,
shrimps to peel.

Stepping away
from red light
wrongs in her midst.

She took
an intermission,
the ever watchful intercessor.

ALAIN DELON

THE TASTE OF FRANCE

Nightcapping

Go,

Intrusive garland of diminished daylight,
a once hot red end of an Alain Delon spliff
now muted and ashy.

settle

Wrapped for presentation,
tar paper packaged lungs,
who breathe as a pretty gesture.

in

What remembers,
a sweaty glass that convalesces,
in a lonesome hand

with,

Belly up to the dark,
suck through chilled teeth,
that old hurt

the name of someone
you should have forgotten by now.

I, Roam at the Ke-o

Winter
sidles
out.

Mango
showers.

Teasing
tartness
from
drupelet
mornings.

She
sweetens
my
unripe
heart.

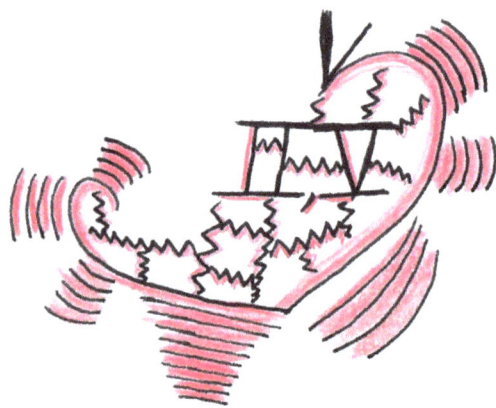

Hangnails or heartbreaks?

Nervously rubbing the right forefinger
around thumbnails,
asymmetrically cut,

in
the unfree haste of morning.

Hands,
one who is right, and who is left remain

uncared for.

For My Girl Friday
on the Occasion of Pchum Ben
&
Columbus Discovering Nada:

The doors of the Killing Fields
opened, monks chanted the Buddha's
Tongue. History's heart rattled.

Remember when we shopped
the market for Monk's Dinner?

Before you threw unbroken Jasmine Rice
to the seven times seven ghost behind.

On the day Columbus Discovered nada.

I will drive where the Geechee were kept in Hell's chains harvested.

A killing field now subdivision and throw Golden Rice
to the seven times seven ghost behind.

To give ghosts full bellies so they send
sweet words to Buddha and Time
to grant us pardon:

Another Sunday on The Hill of Strychnine Trees

You will pull me onto the floor,
and rub my numb extremities with Gold Cup.

I will peel your shrimp.
We will call out "Darling" once again.

My head on your shoulder,
your hand on my back,
I will play with your Potter's Thumb.

Listening to your laugh and breath reincarnate in this now and not the next one.

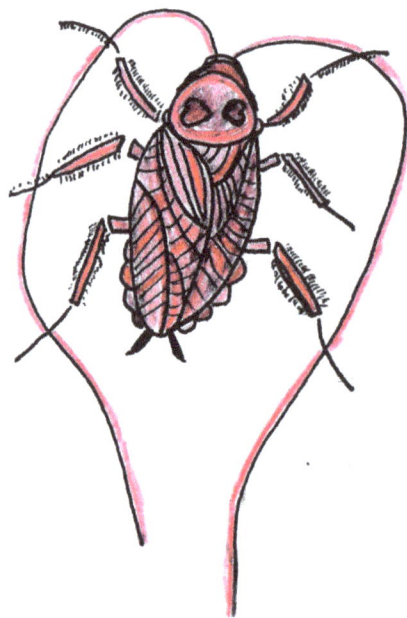

Madame Cockroach Sorts
the Raging Heart of The Fairy Shrimp

Grabbing firmly,
to hate.

Created in
and to be hurled
from My Heart.

Madame Cockroach,
who is fortunately
My Heart,

lullabied
dryly...

"This is the

wrong

address!

What you

fear outside

from here,

away from

you,

and not in

me.

It isn't hate.

'Tis simply, the
Agony of the
Leaves."

Nevertheless,
B.C.F
November 23, 2018

Kind regards to,

Alyshia Quinn

Rev. Jody Gunn

The Yawnties

Mr. and Mrs. O

Dr. and Mrs. Duhon

Dr. Peggy Berry

Dr. Karen Woo

Phoenix Jay

St. Augustine's Episcopal Church

The Bearded Clam

The Sok Family

The Red Fox

My Beloved Community

About

B.C. Farbo's written work has appeared in *Aurora Magazine* where she served as a photography and non-fiction editor. *The Advisor (Phnom Penh)* as a regular featured food and arts essayist, and as a launch contributor for *WikiTribune*.

Her visual work has been featured in *The 23* edited by Marta Rose, and *Hineni Magazine* edited by Jennifer Marie Bartlett for the *43rd New Year's Day Poetry Marathon Reading by The Poetry Project*.

Farbo received her B.A. in Creative Writing from Saint-Mary-of-the-Woods College in 2018. She is currently pursuing an M.A. in Theology with a focus on Theopoetics and the Theological Imagination from Bethany Theological Seminary in Richmond, Indiana.

After being raised in the high deserts of Arizona and hanging her hat in Washington, D.C., Oslo, Norway, Kabul, Afghanistan, New Delhi, India, and Phnom Penh, Cambodia. She currently resides in beautiful downtown Savannah, Georgia.

Cockroach Heart is her first attempt at a book.

www.ingramcontent.com/pod-product-compliance
Lightning Source LLC
Chambersburg PA
CBHW040302100426
42811CB00011B/1337

* 9 7 8 0 5 7 8 4 9 0 9 2 2 *